MODERN ENGINEERING MARVELS

VIRTUAL-REALITY HEADSETS

Valerie Bodden

**Checkerboard
Library**

An Imprint of Abdo Publishing
abdopublishing.com

ABDOPUBLISHING.COM

Published by Abdo Publishing, a division of ABDO, PO Box 398166, Minneapolis, Minnesota 55439. Copyright © 2018 by Abdo Consulting Group, Inc. International copyrights reserved in all countries. No part of this book may be reproduced in any form without written permission from the publisher. Checkerboard Library™ is a trademark and logo of Abdo Publishing.

Printed in the United States of America, North Mankato, Minnesota
062017
092017

THIS BOOK CONTAINS
RECYCLED MATERIALS

Design: Kelly Doudna, Mighty Media, Inc.
Production: Mighty Media, Inc.
Editor: Liz Salzmann
Cover Photograph: Shutterstock
Interior Photographs: Alamy, pp. 21, 25; AP Images, pp. 13, 17, 19, 29 (top); iStockphoto, pp. 5, 26; Maurizio Pesce/Wikimedia Commons, p. 10; othree/Flickr, pp. 15, 29 (bottom); Shutterstock, pp. 1, 9, 18, 27; Steve Jurvetson/Flickr, pp. 11, 28 (bottom right); Wikimedia Commons, pp. 6, 7, 23, 28 (top), 28 (bottom left)

Publisher's Cataloging-in-Publication Data

Names: Bodden, Valerie, author.
Title: Virtual-reality headsets / by Valerie Bodden.
Description: Minneapolis, MN : Abdo Publishing, 2018. | Series: Modern
    engineering marvels.
Identifiers: LCCN 2016962796 | ISBN 9781532110917 (lib. bdg.) |
    ISBN 9781680788761 (ebook)
Subjects: LCSH: Computer simulation-- Juvenile literature. | Virtual reality--
    Juvenile literature. | Electronic apparatus and appliances--Juvenile literature. |
    Technological innovations--Juvenile literature. | Inventions--Juvenile
    literature.
Classification: DDC 600--dc23
LC record available at http://lccn.loc.gov/2016962796

CONTENTS

1 VIRTUAL FIELD TRIP

Your teacher says it is time for a field trip. But you and your classmates don't pile onto a bus. Instead, you strap on big, dark goggles. Instantly, your classroom disappears.

You are standing at the edge of a huge crater. Below you, lava boils and splashes. Smoke and gases billow around you. A low rumble fills the air. Your teacher throws you a rope. You are going down into a volcano! But you are really sitting safely at your desk. This is the power of virtual reality.

Virtual reality, or VR, is the use of **technology** to create a fake world that feels real. Virtual reality's goal is to create telepresence. This is the feeling that you have actually been to another world. To achieve this goal, virtual reality uses immersion. Immersion means that you feel like a virtual world is all around you. Another part of telepresence is interaction. Interaction means you can engage with the virtual world, and the world responds.

It is estimated that 200 million virtual-reality headsets will be sold by 2020!

People have been working on virtual reality for a long time. And some of the VR devices available today are amazing! While a virtual field trip into a volcano isn't quite possible yet, it may be closer than you think!

The earliest attempts at immersion were in the 1800s. Some artists at that time created huge paintings called cycloramas. These 360-degree paintings surrounded viewers. People felt like they had stepped into the scene of the painting.

Also in the 1800s, the stereoscope was invented. British scientist Charles Wheatstone created it in 1838. The stereoscope had two mirrors. Each mirror reflected a slightly different version of the same image toward the viewer. The viewer's brain processed the two images as one **3-D** picture.

In 1931, Edward Link patented the Link Trainer flight **simulator** to train pilots. Each simulator was a mock airplane that a pilot sat inside. As the pilot moved the controls, motors tilted the simulator.

Later flight simulators included films of scenes pilots

TECH TIDBIT

A handheld stereoscope called the View-Master was invented in 1939.

Many countries used Link Trainer simulators to train pilots during World War II.

might see out of airplane windows. The pilots viewed films while in the **simulator**. They could practice reacting to different situations. Cycloramas, stereoscopes, and flight simulators didn't achieve virtual reality. But they were steps in the right direction. And new developments were right around the corner.

HEAD-MOUNTED DISPLAYS

The next big step in virtual reality was invented in 1957. It was the Sensorama, developed by US filmmaker Morton Heilig. This was a large cabinet with a chair in front of it. A viewer put his or her head inside the cabinet. A screen inside the cabinet showed a **3-D** movie. Speakers provided **stereo** sound. Electric fans blew related scents into the cabinet. The viewer's chair shook with the movie's action. The Sensorama provided a sense of immersion, but its large size kept it from becoming popular.

Around the same time, other VR developers created smaller displays. They were called head-mounted displays (HMDs) because they fit on users' heads. Headsight was the first HMD. It was a helmet with a video screen for each eye. The video screens were linked to a remote camera. The user could turn his or her head to direct the camera.

In 1968, US inventor Ivan Sutherland created the Sword of Damocles. It was the first HMD for virtual programs. This HMD was very heavy. So, a mechanical arm held it suspended from

The first HMDs paved the way for modern virtual-reality headsets.

the ceiling. A computer connected to the HMD showed simple **3-D** outlines of rooms and objects to the wearer. The HMD tracked the user's head movements. The view changed as the user looked around. But the images were not realistic.

In the 1980s, the US military was looking for more realistic flight **simulators**. This led to the Super Cockpit. Military engineer Thomas Furness invented it in 1986.

The Super Cockpit was an HMD that let pilots see the real world and the virtual world at the same time. The simulation changed based on the pilot's actions. The HMD even had voice-activated controls. But it was expensive. With a price tag of $1 million, only one was ever built.

Other VR pioneers worked on games. They wanted to make video games featuring virtual worlds that players could enter. In 1984, game developer Jaron Lanier formed the company VPL.

TECH TIDBIT

Using a VR headset for long periods can cause **nausea** and dizziness. Developers are working on ways to reduce these effects.

Jaron Lanier *(left)* was the first person to use the term "virtual reality."

VPL made HMDs that looked like goggles. Wires ran from the goggles to computers that ran the VR games.

VPL also invented the DataGlove. Sensors in the glove tracked the user's hand movements. A user could move objects in a virtual world with his or her hand. By the late 1980s, VPL had created Reality Built for Two. This was the first virtual program for two users. The users could share and interact with a virtual world. And they could interact with each other in that virtual world.

By 1991, some **arcades** began to feature VR games. Many of these games were created by British company Virtuality Group. Several players could strap on VR goggles. Then they could play the same game at the same time. Some people thought virtual reality would take off after this. But the **technology** was still expensive, so few arcades could afford to purchase them.

The technology was not yet advanced enough, either. Computers were slow and the graphics were of low quality. This made images appear choppy. There was also a delay between the time users turned their heads and the time the screen responded. This delay was known as latency.

In 1995, video game company Nintendo tried to fix these issues. It released the Virtual Boy. Virtual Boy was a wearable **3-D** video game console. It cost $180, which was less than other devices. But still it did not sell well. Users said it was uncomfortable. And its graphics were unrealistic. All images were in red and black.

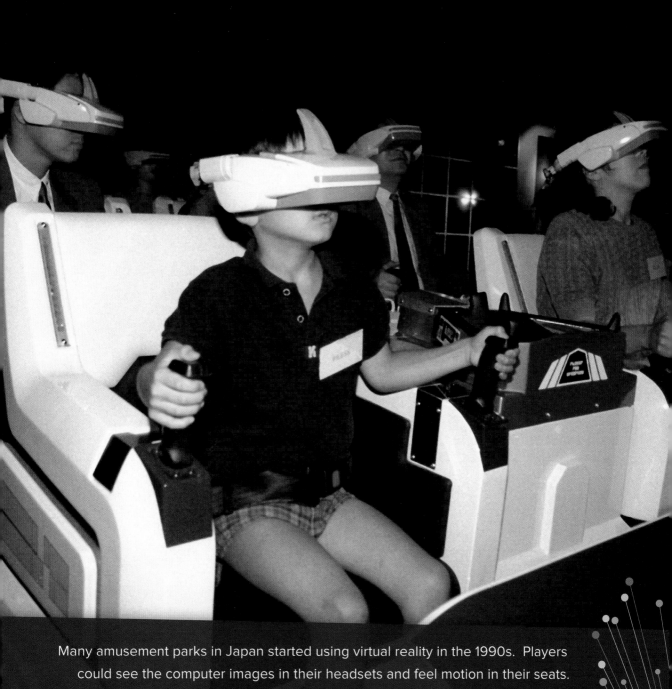

Many amusement parks in Japan started using virtual reality in the 1990s. Players could see the computer images in their headsets and feel motion in their seats.

NEW VIRTUAL LIFE

By the early 2000s, many people thought virtual reality was dead. But developers continued to work on VR products. By this time, computers had become smaller, faster, and more powerful. This led to the development of smartphones.

Smartphones could fit in a user's hand or pocket. They had high-resolution screens. The phones also had sensors to detect motion. Smartphone screens, sensors, and **processors** could be adapted for virtual reality.

One HMD that used a smartphone was Google Cardboard. Google released it in 2014. This device was a pair of cardboard goggles. Users placed their smartphones into the goggles. The goggles gave the users a 360-degree view of a virtual **environment**. When the user turned, the view shifted.

Other companies released different types of VR devices for smartphones. These devices used the same **technique** as early stereoscopes. The goggles split the user's phone into two

Most Google Cardboard viewers are less than $25. These viewers are used with smartphones that have the Google Cardboard app installed on them.

screens. Each screen showed a different version of the same image. The brain interpreted the image as **3-D**.

The year 2016 brought virtual reality's biggest breakthroughs. That year, several new HMDs hit the market. One that received much attention was Oculus Rift. This device was created by US inventor Palmer Luckey.

In 2012, Luckey had raised $2.5 million through the fund-raising website Kickstarter. He used the money to start his company, Oculus VR, and fund development of his HMD. Luckey called his HMD Oculus Rift. The device did not use a smartphone. Instead, it was connected to a computer.

Luckey wanted to sell his HMD to a **technology** developer. He showed Oculus Rift **prototypes** to several companies. In 2014, social media company Facebook purchased Luckey's company and HMD for $2 billion. Oculus devices went on sale to the public in 2016.

Oculus Rift solved many of the problems of earlier HMDs. Sensors in the device detected head rotation. **Infrared** cameras tracked the head's position. These tracking devices reduced

Oculus also sells special controllers, earphones, and sensors for an

Oculus Rift's latency to about 40 milliseconds. So, the delay was barely noticeable to users.

Also, earlier VR headsets had shown a small image that looked far away. But Oculus Rift had a wide view that filled the user's entire field of vision. This made users feel like they were surrounded by the virtual world.

Another HMD released in 2016 was the HTC Vive. Like Oculus, Vive worked with a computer. But Vive also had sensors that could be mounted around a room. The sensors mapped the player's location and sent this data to the computer. This allowed players more freedom to move around. There are more than 200 games that can be played with HTC Vive. These games let players do almost anything, from shoot basketballs to chase zombies.

People attending the 2016 Untold Festival could try HTC Vive headsets. The Untold Festival is a music festival held in Romania each August.

PALMER LUCKEY

Palmer Luckey was born in Long Beach, California, in 1992. From a young age, he loved computers and video games. At age 17, Luckey started working on Oculus Rift. *Oculus* is the Latin word for "eye." And *Rift* stands for the rift, or separation, between the virtual and real worlds. Although he sold Oculus to Facebook, Luckey remained at the company. He is credited with bringing virtual reality into the twenty-first century.

Luckey was awarded the Royal Photographic Society Progress Medal in 2016 for his contributions to imaging development.

The Oculus Rift and the HTC Vive are not the only HMDs available. Other **technology** companies have released or are developing their own HMDs. The market for VR products is growing quickly.

7 VIRTUAL FUN

Today, virtual reality is used largely by people who play video and computer games. VR games allow players to step into the action. Entertainment company Six Flags even added a VR game to roller coasters in eight Six Flags theme parks. The game is called Rage of the Gargoyles. To play the game, riders wear HMDs and shoot virtual monsters.

VR movies and TV shows are also starting to appear. Viewers watching a virtual movie feel like they are in the movie's world. Instead of just seeing what's on a screen in front of them, they can turn and see what's happening in all directions. Some VR films even let viewers affect what happens in the movie.

Virtual reality can be used to teach people too. The *New York Times* offers VR videos to enhance some of its news stories. These can be viewed using Google Cardboard. The VR videos include experiencing the campaign trail and seeing through the eyes of a **refugee**. Some schools use virtual reality to teach students about the Egyptian Pyramids, outer space, and more.

Oculus offers many free games, movies, and videos. Most virtual-reality games are about the same price as regular video games!

People can also use virtual reality to connect with faraway friends or relatives. Each person can make an avatar. An avatar is a computer version of a person. The avatars can meet in a virtual room to talk, watch a movie, and even play games.

8 VIRTUAL WORK

Virtual reality isn't only for fun and games. It can be used for work too. Pilots continue to train using VR programs. Soldiers use virtual reality to prepare for combat. Doctors use virtual reality to practice surgeries.

Virtual reality is also used to create new products. Car designers can create and test virtual cars. That way, they can fix problems before the car is ever built. Virtual reality has even been used to design submarines!

Police officers have started to use virtual reality to investigate crime scenes. They use special cameras to make virtual models of crime scenes. Then, investigators can tour the virtual crime scene to look for clues. This keeps the crime scene free from **contamination**. It also allows officers to later view the scene exactly as it was. And they can view it at the police station or wherever they happen to be.

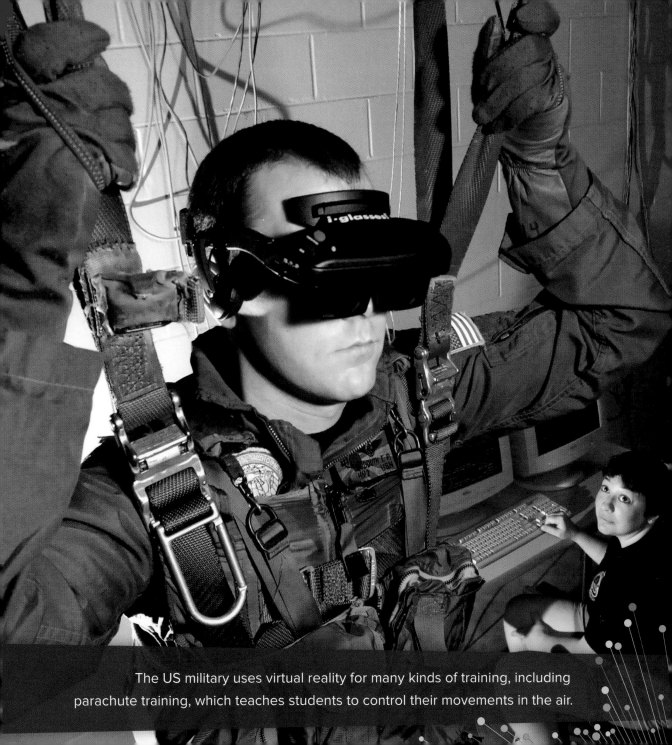

The US military uses virtual reality for many kinds of training, including parachute training, which teaches students to control their movements in the air.

It's likely that someday, millions of people will regularly use virtual reality. They might hang out in virtual cities. They could visit the doctor virtually. People might even travel virtually to sporting events and concerts. Everyone could have the best seat!

In the future, HMDs will likely contain everything users need to run virtual programs. This means they will not have to be connected to computers or smartphones. Some designers think one day people won't need HMDs at all. Instead, tiny light sources will project virtual **3-D** images right into people's eyes!

Developers are also working on eye and body tracking systems. These will allow users to control the virtual world using only their hands or eyes. They won't need to wear goggles or gloves. Users' avatars will reflect their facial expressions. Someday, VR systems might even be able to read people's thoughts and send thoughts to their friends.

Beyond virtual reality lies **augmented** reality. Unlike virtual reality, augmented reality does not block out the real

AGATHE is a tool being developed in France that allows patients to receive virtual therapy and rehabilitation.

world. Instead, it layers virtual objects on top of the real world. For example, people could put virtual chess boards on their kitchen tables. They could play the game but still be aware of the real world. **Augmented** reality glasses are already being developed. Someday, there might even be **augmented** reality contact lenses.

Augmented reality could be used to help people perform **complex** tasks. It could help someone do electrical work by displaying **diagrams** on a wall to show the wires underneath. Similarly, it could provide information to help a doctor perform a difficult surgery.

Virtual reality has come a long way from cycloramas and stereoscopes. There have been plenty of difficulties along the way. But with all of today's advances, the virtual future is coming fast!

Pokémon Go is an example of augmented reality. Players can hold up their smartphones or tablets and see Pokémon characters in front of them!

VR HEADSET

Today's VR headsets contain a lot of technology in a small space.

TRACKING SENSORS
Sensors inside the headset track the user's head movements. The display changes as the user moves.

LENSES
VR headsets have two lenses. Each lens displays a high-quality screen. Like early stereoscopes, each screen shows a slightly different image. The user's brain combines the images to see it in **3-D**.

HEAD STRAP
HMDs weigh about one pound (0.45 kg). The head strap keeps the headset from sliding down.

HEADPHONES
Headphones provide **stereo** audio. Sounds seem to come from all around the user.

CABLE
The cable connects the headset to a computer. The computer runs the VR software.

TECH TIMELINE

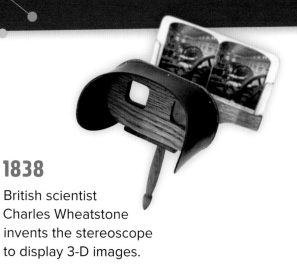

1838
British scientist Charles Wheatstone invents the stereoscope to display 3-D images.

1968
Ivan Sutherland develops the Sword of Damocles, a heavy headset that hangs from the ceiling.

1931
Edward Link patents the Link Trainer flight simulator.

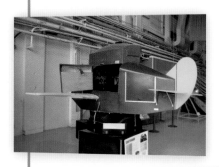

1957
Morton Heilig develops the Sensorama, which combines 3-D video and sound with smell and movement.

1984
Jaron Lanier forms technology company VPL.

1986
Thomas Furness develops the Super Cockpit flight simulator.

2012
Palmer Luckey uses Kickstarter to raise money to develop Oculus Rift.

1995
Nintendo releases Virtual Boy.

2014
Google releases Google Cardboard. Facebook purchases Oculus from Palmer Luckey.

2016
Oculus Rift and HTC Vive are released.

GLOSSARY

arcade–a business in which electronic game machines, such as pinball, can be played for entertainment.

augment–to add to something.

complex–having many parts, details, ideas, or functions.

contamination–the process of making unfit for use by adding something harmful or unpleasant.

diagram–a drawing or graphic that explains a concept using images, arrows, and other symbols.

environment–all the surroundings that affect the growth and well-being of a living thing.

infrared–relating to energy transmitted by waves, which can be felt as heat.

nausea–an upset stomach or the feeling of needing to throw up.

processor–the part of a computer that processes data.

prototype–an early model of a product on which future versions can be modeled.

refugee–a person who flees to another country for safety and protection.

simulator–a device that imitates a real experience.

stereo–a way of playing recorded sound so that it comes from multiple directions and is more like live sound.

technique (tehk-NEEK)–a method or style in which something is done.

technology–a capability given by the practical application of knowledge.

3-D–having length, width, and height and taking up space.

INDEX